Unit 1: Seasons

Let's learn about:

- ☐ Spring
- ☐ Summer
- ☐ Fall/Autumn
- ☐ Winter

There are four seasons.
Which season is it now?

Let's talk about spring!

 Draw at least three spring activities or things.

- In spring, I can...

○ _____

○ _____

○ _____

○ _____

Brainstorm about spring.

Use your dictionary.

Q When is spring in your country?

A Spring in my country is _____

_____

_____

Q What event do you have in the spring?

A We have _____ in the spring.

_____

Tell me more.
When is it?
What do you
do/eat/see?

_____

Q What do you like to (see / eat / play / do / ☐) in the spring?

A ① I like to _____

_____

_____

Q Why do you like it?

A ② Because... _____

> I like to see cherry blossoms.

_____

_____

Challenge

Q Choose a question and check the ☐.

☐ What is your favorite spring flower? Why?

☐ Do you like spring? Why or why not?

☐ What is your best spring memory?
Tell me more.

A ③ _____

_____

_____

_____

Spring

Make a script for your presentation.

My name is   .

① _____

_____

_____

② _____

_____

_____

_____

③ _____

_____

_____

_____

_____

I thought your presentation was...

(awesome) · (great) · (nice) · (interesting)

Circle one and sign.

Signature:_____

Teacher's Comments:

☐Eye Contact ☐Clear Voice ☐Smile ☐Gesture ☐Speed

5

Let's talk about summer!

Draw at least three summer activities or things.

✎ *Hint* Write about your picture. What can you do? What can you see?

○ In summer, I can...

○ _____

○ _____

○ _____

○ _____

Brainstorm about summer.

Use your dictionary. *Hint*

Q ─ When is summer in your country?

A ─ Summer in my country is _____

_____

_____

Q ─ What event do you have in the summer?

A ─ We have _____   in the summer.

_____

Tell me more.
When is it?
What do you
do/eat/see?

_____

Hint

7

Q What do you like to (see / eat / play / do / [   ]) in the summer?

A ① I like to _____

_____

_____

Q Why do you like it?

A ② Because... _____

_____

_____

Challenge

Q Choose a question and check the ☐.

☐ What is your favorite summer fruit? Why?

☐ Do you like summer? Why or why not?

☐ What is your best summer memory?
Tell me more.

A ③ _____

_____

_____

_____

Summer

Make a script for your presentation.

My name is _____ .

①

_____

_____

②

_____

_____

_____

③

_____

_____

_____

> I like to catch fish and eat watermelon in the summer.

I thought your presentation was...

(fantastic) · (good) · (well done) · (superb)

Circle one and sign.

Signature:_____

Teacher's Comments:

☐Eye Contact ☐Clear Voice ☐Smile ☐Gesture ☐Speed

9

Let's talk about fall/autumn*!

 Draw at least three autumn activities or things.

Fall and **autumn** have the same meaning. Which will you use, fall or autumn?

Write about your picture. What can you do? What can you see?

- In autumn, I can...

- _____

- _____

- _____

- _____

Brainstorm about fall.

Use your dictionary.

Q — When is autumn in your country?

A — Fall in my country is _____

_____

_____

Q — What event do you have in the fall?

A — We have _____ in the fall.

_____

Tell me more. When is it? What do you do/eat/see?

_____

11

Q What do you like to (see / eat / play / do / ⬚) in the fall?

①A I like to _____

_____

_____

Q Why do you like it?

②A Because... _____

_____

_____

Challenge

Q Choose a question and check the ☐.

☐ What is your favorite fall vegetable? Why?

☐ Do you like autumn? Why or why not?

☐ What is your best autumn memory?
Tell me more.

③A _____

_____

_____

_____

Fall/Autumn

Make a script for your presentation.

My name is _____ .

① _____
_____
_____

② _____
_____
_____
_____

③ _____
_____
_____
_____

_____

I thought your presentation was...

(amazing) · (super) · (cool) · (wonderful)

Hint
Circle one
and sign.

Signature: _____

Teacher's Comments:

☐Eye Contact ☐Clear Voice ☐Smile ☐Gesture ☐Speed

13

Let's talk about winter!

Draw at least three winter activities or things.

Write about your picture. What can you do? What can you see?

- In winter, I can...

- _____

- _____

- _____

- _____

Brainstorm about winter.

Use your dictionary.

Q When is winter in your country?

A Winter in my country is _____

_____

_____

Q What event do you have in the winter?

A We have _____ in the winter.

_____

Tell me more.
When is it?
What do you
do/eat/see?

Santa brings me presents
on Christmas morning.

15

Q What do you like to (see / eat / play / do / [   ]) in the winter?

A ① I like to _____

_____

_____

Q Why do you like it?

A ② Because... _____

_____

_____

Challenge

Q Choose a question and check the ☐.

☐ What is your favorite winter sport? Why?

☐ Do you like winter? Why or why not?

☐ What is your best winter memory?
Tell me more.

A ③ _____

_____

_____

Winter

Make a script for your presentation.

My name is _____ .

① _____

_____

_____

② _____

_____

_____

_____

③ _____

_____

_____

_____

I thought your presentation was...

(terrific) · (excellent) · (unique) · (marvelous)

Hint
Circle one
and sign.

Signature:_____

Teacher's Comments:

☐Eye Contact ☐Clear Voice ☐Smile ☐Gesture ☐Speed

17

Review

Q What is your favorite season? Why?

A _____

_____

_____

_____

My favorite season is winter, because I like playing in the snow.

Look it up. Research your favorite season and answer the questions below.

① **Q** How's the weather during your favorite season?

A _____

_____

② **Q** What fruits and vegetables grow during your favorite season?

A _____

_____

Unit 2: My Home

Let's learn about:

☐ My Country

☐ My Prefecture

☐ My City

☐ My School

There are 7 continents.
There are 195 countries.
There are over 10,000 big cities.
Wow! That's a lot.

Let's talk about your country!

 Draw at least three famous things from your country.

I'm from the United States.
Hot dogs and football
are from the U.S.

Write about your picture.

● My country is famous for...

● _____

● _____

● _____

● _____

Brainstorm about your country.

Use your dictionary

Q What is the biggest city in your country?

A _____ is the biggest

city in _____

Q What do you like about your country? Why?

A _____

_____

_____

_____

Hint Write your country in the [____].
Then research your country and answer the questions.

Q What food is popular in [_____] ? Why?

A ① I think _____

_____

_____

Q What sport is popular in [_____] ? Why?

A ② I think _____

_____

_____

Challenge

Q Choose a question and check the ☐.

☐ What's your favorite food from [_____] ?

☐ What's your favorite place in [_____] ?

☐ What's your favorite event in [_____] ?

A ③ _____

_____

_____

Tell me more! Why is it your favorite?

Hint

22

My Country

Make a script for your presentation.

My name is _____ .

① _____

_____

② _____

_____

_____

③ _____

_____

_____

I thought your presentation was...

awesome · great · nice · interesting

Circle one
and sign.

Signature: _____

Teacher's Comments:

☐Eye Contact ☐Clear Voice ☐Smile ☐Gesture ☐Speed

Let's talk about your prefecture!

✎ Draw at least three famous things from your prefecture.

Hint Write about your picture.

- My prefecture is famous for...

- _____

- _____

- _____

- _____

Brainstorm about your prefecture.

Use your dictionary. *Hint*

Q ⟨ What is the biggest city in your prefecture?

A ⟨ _____ is the biggest

city in _____

Q ⟨ What do you like about your prefecture? Why?

A ⟨ _____

_____

_____

_____

25

Write your prefecture in the ☐.
Then research your prefecture and answer the questions.

Q What food is popular in [＿＿＿]? Why?

① **A** _____

_____

_____

Q What temples, shrines, buildings, etc., are popular in [＿＿＿]? Why?

② **A** _____

_____

_____

Challange

America has states. I'm from the state of Colorado. My favorite food from Colorado is the Denver omelette.

Q Choose a question and check the ☐.

☐ What's your favorite food from [＿＿＿]?

☐ What's your favorite place in [＿＿＿]?

☐ What's your favorite event in [＿＿＿]?

③ **A** _____

_____

Tell me more! Why is it your favorite?

_____

My Prefecture

Make a script for your presentation.

My name is _____ .

①
_____
_____

②
_____
_____
_____

③
_____
_____
_____

I thought your presentation was...

(fantastic) · (good) · (well done) · (superb)

Hint (Circle one and sign.)

Signature:_____

Teacher's Comments:

☐Eye Contact ☐Clear Voice ☐Smile ☐Gesture ☐Speed

Let's talk about your city!

Draw at least three famous things from your city.

✏️ *Hint* Write about your picture.

Use your dictionary. *Hint*

○ My city is famous for...

○ _____

○ _____

○ _____

○ _____

Brainstorm about your city.

Think about places: schools, police stations, train stations, fire stations, convenience stores. What else is there?

Q What can we see in every city?

A Every city has _____

_____

Q What do you think is the most important place in your city? Why?

A I think _____

is the most important place,

because _____

_____

I think the park is the most important place, because I can play there.

29

Q What event is popular in [_____] ?
Why?

①
A <u>I think</u> _____

_____

_____

Q What do you like about [_____] ? Why?

②
A <u>I think</u> _____

_____

_____

Challenge

Q Choose a question and check the ☐.

☐ What's your favorite place to go in [_____] ?

☐ What do you think of [_____] ?

☐ Do you want to live in [_____] forever?

Tell me more!
Hint

③
A _____

_____

_____

30

My City

Make a script for your presentation.

My name is _____ .

① _____

_____

_____

② _____

_____

_____

_____

③ _____

_____

_____

_____

_____

I thought your presentation was...

(amazing) · (super) · (cool) · (wonderful)

Hint

Circle one and sign.

Signature: _____

Teacher's Comments:

☐Eye Contact ☐Clear Voice ☐Smile ☐Gesture ☐Speed

Let's talk about your school!

Draw at least three subjects you learn in school.

Write about your picture.

- In school, I learn about...

- _____

- _____

- _____

- _____

Brainstorm about your school.

Use your dictionary.

Q — What do you eat at school?

A — We eat _____

_____

Q — What do you like about your school? Why?

A — _____

_____

_____

33

Hint Write your school in the ☐ .
Then research your school and answer the questions.

Q What is the most popular school lunch at

[   ] ? Why?

① **A** I think _____

_____

Q What is the most popular subject at

[   ] ? Why?

② **A** I think _____

_____

Challenge

Q Choose a question and check the ☐ .

☐ What is your favorite subject? Why?

☐ Who is your favorite teacher? Why?

☐ What is your favorite event at [   ] ?
Why?

③ **A** _____

_____

_____

My School

Make a script for your presentation.

My name is _____ .

① _____

_____

_____

② _____

_____

_____

_____

③ _____

_____

_____

_____

_____

I thought your presentation was...

(terrific) · (excellent) · (unique) · (marvelous)

Hint

Circle one and sign.

Signature: _____

Teacher's Comments:

I go to Owl School. My favorite event is the mouse chase. We catch mice in the forest.

☐Eye Contact ☐Clear Voice ☐Smile ☐Gesture ☐Speed

Review

Q Where would you like to travel in your country? Why?

A _____

_____

_____

_____

I would like to travel to Hawaii, because I want to see volcano beaches.

Look it up. Research the place you would like to visit. Then, answer the questions below.

① Q What famous places are there?

A _____

_____

② Q What famous food can you eat there?

A _____

_____

Unit 3: Nature

Let's learn about:

- ☐ The Desert
- ☐ The Mountains
- ☐ The Jungle
- ☐ The Ocean

Nature is amazing. I live in a forest. There are many trees in the forest.

Let's talk about the desert!

Draw a desert with plants and animals.

- ## The desert has...

- _____

- _____

- _____

- _____

Brainstorm about the desert.

Q How's the weather in the desert?

A The desert is _____

_____

_____

Q Do you like the desert? Why or why not?

A _____

_____

_____

_____

The desert is too hot for me.

Hint Choose one desert animal. Write that animal in the ☐ below. Research the animal. Then answer the questions.

Q What do ☐ eat? How do they get it?

① A _____

_____

_____

Q What can ☐ do? Tell me more.

② A _____

_____

_____

Challenge

Q Choose a question and check the ☐.

☐ Where do ☐ sleep?

☐ What do ☐ look like?

☐ Why did you choose ☐ ?

③ A _____

_____

_____

Desert Animals

Make a script for your presentation.

My name is _____ .

① _____

_____

② _____

_____

_____

③ _____

_____

_____

_____

I thought your presentation was...

(awesome) · (great) · (nice) · (interesting)

Circle one and sign.

Signature: _____

Teacher's Comments:

☐Eye Contact ☐Clear Voice ☐Smile ☐Gesture ☐Speed

Let's talk about the mountains!

 Draw the mountains with plants and animals.

Some mountains have tall trees and cold rivers.

✏️ Write about your picture.

• **The mountains have...**

What plants and animals did you draw?

○ _____

○ _____

○ _____

○ _____

Brainstorm about the mountains.

Use your dictionary.

List the mountains you know.

Q What are two mountains you know?

A <u>I know</u> _____

_____

_____

Q Do you like the mountains? Why or why not?

A _____

_____

_____

43

Hint Choose one mountain animal. Write that animal in the [ ] below. Research the animal. Then answer the questions.

Q What do [ ] eat? How do they get it?

①**A** _____

_____

_____

Q What can [ ] do? Tell me more.

②**A** _____

_____

_____

Challenge

Q Choose a question and check the ☐.

☐ Where do [ ] sleep?

☐ What do [ ] look like?

☐ Why did you choose [ ] ?

③**A** _____

_____

_____

_____

Presentation

Mountain Animals

Make a script for your presentation.

My name is _____.

① _____

_____

_____

② _____

_____

_____

_____

③ _____

_____

_____

_____

I thought your presentation was...

fantastic · good · well done · superb

Hint

Circle one and sign.

Signature: _____

Teacher's Comments:

☐Eye Contact ☐Clear Voice ☐Smile ☐Gesture ☐Speed

Let's talk about the jungle!

Draw a jungle with plants and animals.

Write about your picture.

The jungle has...

What plants and animals did you draw?

• _____

• _____

• _____

• _____

Brainstorm about the jungle.

Use your dictionary.

Q How's the weather in the jungle?

A The jungle is _____

_____

_____

Q Do you like the jungle? Why or why not?

A _____

_____

_____

_____

There are unique animals there!

Hint Choose one jungle animal. Write that animal in the ☐ below.
Research the animal. Then answer the questions.

Q What do [ ] eat? How do they get it?

① A _____

_____

_____

Q What can [ ] do? Tell me more.

② A _____

_____

_____

Challenge

Q Choose a question and check the ☐.

☐ Where do [ ] sleep?

☐ What do [ ] look like?

☐ Why did you choose [ ] ?

③ A _____

_____

_____

_____

Presentation

Jungle Animals

Make a script for your presentation.

My name is _____ .

① _____

_____

_____

② _____

_____

_____

_____

③ _____

_____

_____

_____

I thought your presentation was...

amazing · super · cool · wonderful

Hint Circle one and sign.

Signature: _____

Teacher's Comments:

☐Eye Contact ☐Clear Voice ☐Smile ☐Gesture ☐Speed

49

Let's talk about the ocean!

Draw the ocean with plants and animals.

● The ocean has...

Hint What plants and animals did you draw?

○ _____

○ _____

○ _____

○ _____

Brainstorm about the ocean.

Hint Use your dictionary.

Q How many oceans do you know?

Hint Check the map on p. 68-69.

A I know _____ oceans: _____

_____

_____

Q Do you like the ocean? Why or why not?

A _____

_____

_____

_____

I can't swim!

Choose one ocean animal. Write that animal in the ☐ below. Research the animal. Then answer the questions.

Q What do [_____] eat? How do they get it?

① **A** _____

_____

_____

Q What can [_____] do? Tell me more.

② **A** _____

_____

_____

Tiger sharks have stripes or spots. I think that's cool!

Challenge

Q Choose a question and check the ☐.

☐ Where do [_____] sleep?

☐ What do [_____] look like?

☐ Why did you choose [_____]?

③ **A** _____

_____

_____

Ocean Animals

Make a script for your presentation.

My name is _____ .

① _____

_____

_____

② _____

_____

_____

_____

③ _____

_____

_____

_____

I thought your presentation was...

terrific · excellent · unique · marvelous

Hint
Circle one
and sign.

Signature: _____

Teacher's Comments:

☐Eye Contact ☐Clear Voice ☐Smile ☐Gesture ☐Speed

Review

Q What is your favorite place in nature? Why?

A _____

_____

_____

_____

> My favorite place in nature is the jungle, because many different animals live in the jungle.

Look it up. Research your favorite place in nature. Then, answer the questions below.

① **Q** Where is the biggest jungle / mountain / desert / ocean? What is it called?

A _____

_____

② **Q** Think about the desert / mountains / jungle / ocean. What can you do there?

A _____

_____

Review

Let's practice speaking, reading and writing.

Section 1: ☐ Seasons Interview

☐ Letter from Jack

☐ Letter to Jack

Section 2: ☐ My Home Interview

☐ Letter from Bao

☐ Letter to Bao

Section 3: ☐ Nature Interview

☐ Letter from Maria

☐ Letter to Maria

☐ World Map

Can you find your country on the map?

Interview a friend using the script below.
Remember to make eye contact, speak clearly, and react to what they say.

下のスクリプトを使い、友だちにインタビューします。
相手の目を見ながら、はっきりと話し、忘れずにリアクションをしましょう

Hello. May I ask you some questions about seasons?

Sure.

What do you like to see in the spring?

I like to see _____ in the spring.

React:

Sounds beautiful / I want to see that / Wow.
What do you like to eat in the summer?

I like to eat _____ in the summer.

Continue to the next page!

React:

Sounds delicious / I want to try that / Yummy .
What do you like to play in the fall?

I like to play _____ in the fall.

React:

Sounds fun / I want to play that / Nice .
What do you like to do in the winter?

I like to _____ in the winter.

React:

Sounds interesting / I want to do that / Cool .
Thanks for answering my questions.

You're welcome. Now can I ask you some questions about seasons?

Now switch roles!

1 Let's read a letter from Jack.

Write your name here.

Dear _____,

    My name is Jack. I'm from England.

    I like spring, because spring is bright and colorful. I like to see cherry blossoms in the spring, because I like to take pictures of flowers.

    Which season do you like?

    When is spring in your country?

Sincerely,
Jack

Reading Comprehension Questions

We always start with "Dear" and finish with "Sincerely, ～."

Q Where is Jack from?

Q What season does he like?

Q What does he like to do in the spring?

Let's write a letter to Jack.

Dear Jack,

_____

_____

_____

_____

_____

Tell me more.

Sincerely,

_____

Q: Can you find England on the map on pages 68-69? Color England blue.

England is in Europe.

Hint

Interview a friend using the script below.
Remember to make eye contact, speak clearly, and react to what they say.

下のスクリプトを使い、友だちにインタビューします。
相手の目を見ながら、はっきりと話し、忘れずにリアクションをしましょう。

 Hello. May I ask you some questions about your home?

 Sure.

 Where are you from? What country, prefecture, and city?

I'm from _____.

React:
 Me, too / That's nice / I see .
What food is popular in your country?

_____ **is popular**
in _____.

 Continue to the next page!

React:
A
Sounds delicious / Yummy
/ I want to try that .
What event is popular in your prefecture?

B
_____ is popular
in _____ .

React:
A
Sounds fun / Neat / I want to see that .
What place is popular in your city?

B
_____ is popular
in _____ .

React:
A
Sounds interesting / Cool
/ I want to go there .
Thanks for answering my questions.

B
You're welcome. Now can I ask you some questions about your home?

Now switch roles!

61

2 Let's read a letter from Bao.

Write your name here.
Hint

Dear _____,

　Hi! My name is Bao. I'm Chinese. There are 333 prefectures in China. How many prefectures does your country have? China has a lot of delicious food.

　The most popular meal is huǒguō. Huǒguō in English is "hotpot." Do you have hotpot in your country?

　A famous place in China is the Forbidden City. It is the largest palace in the world. But my favorite place in China is the Great Wall of China, because it's over 2,300 years old!

　Can you tell me about your country?

I hope to hear from you soon,
Bao

Reading Comprehension Questions

Q What is a famous place in China? Why is it famous?

Q What is over 2,300 years old?

Q Do you like hotpot? Why or why not?

Let's write a letter to Bao.

Dear Bao,

_____

_____

_____

_____

_____

_____ Tell me more.

Sincerely,

_____

Q Can you find China on the map on pages 68-69? Color China red.

China is in Asia.

Section 3 — Nature Interview

Interview a friend using the script below.
Remember to make eye contact, speak clearly, and react to what they say.

下のスクリプトを使い、友だちにインタビューします。
相手の目を見ながら、はっきりと話し、忘れずにリアクションをしましょう。

 A: Hello. May I ask you some questions about nature?

B: Sure.

 A: Which do you like best: the desert, the mountains, the jungle or the ocean? Why?

B: I like the _____ best, because
_____.

React:
 A: Me, too / That's nice / I see .
What animals can you find there?

B: _____
live in the _____.

Continue to the next page!

64

React:

A: Wow! / Cool / I didn't know that . What can _____ do?

Hint: Say one animal from your friend's answer.

B: _____ can _____ .

React:

A: Amazing / Really? / That's interesting . What do _____ eat?

B: _____ eat _____ .

React:

A: That's gross / Neat / I eat that, too . Thanks for answering my questions.

B: You're welcome. Now can I ask you some questions about nature?

Now switch roles!

3 Let's read a letter from Maria.

Dear _____ Hint

Write your name here.

Hello! My name is Maria. I'm from Brazil. Have you ever been to Brazil? Brazil is in South America. The largest jungle in the world is also in South America. The jungle is called the Amazon rainforest.

Many animals live in the Amazon. I think the pink dolphin is the cutest animal in the jungle. Pink dolphins live in the Amazon River. They can weigh 181 kilograms. Wow! I think anacondas are the scariest animals in the jungle. They are the largest snakes in the world. They can eat deer!

Tell me about the animals near you.

Maria

Reading Comprehension Questions

Q Where is the Amazon rainforest?

_____

Q Where do pink dolphins live?

_____

Q Do you think anacondas are scary? Why or why not?

_____

Let's write a letter to Maria.

Dear Maria,

_____

_____

_____

_____

_____

                      Tell me more.

         Sincerely,

        _____

Q: Can you find Brazil on the map on pages 68-69? Color Brazil green.

Brazil is in South America.

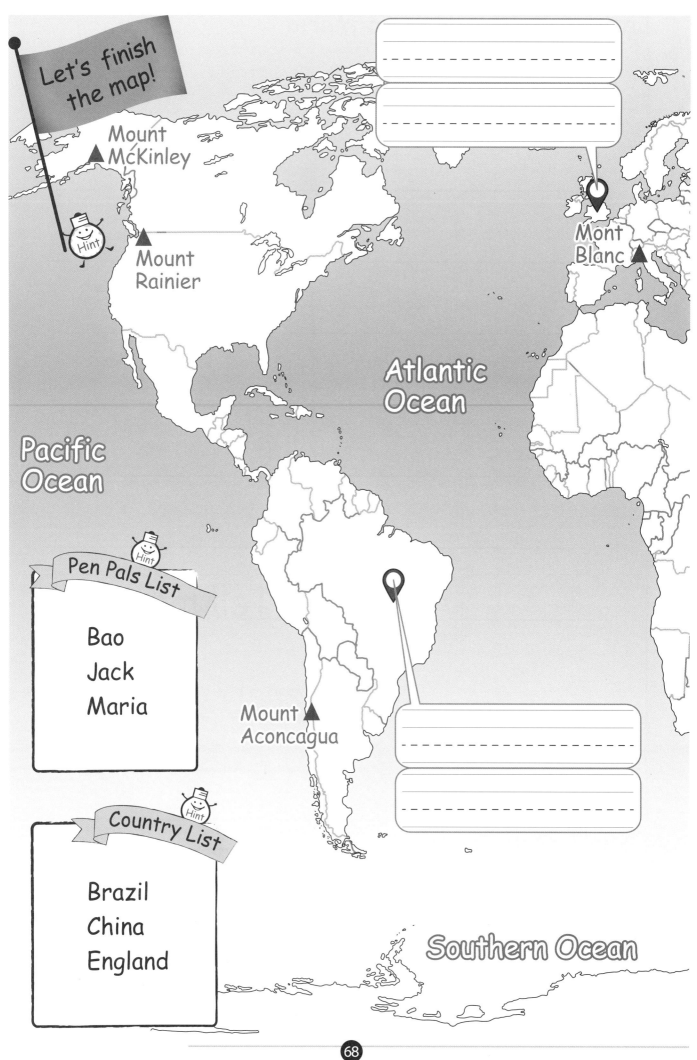

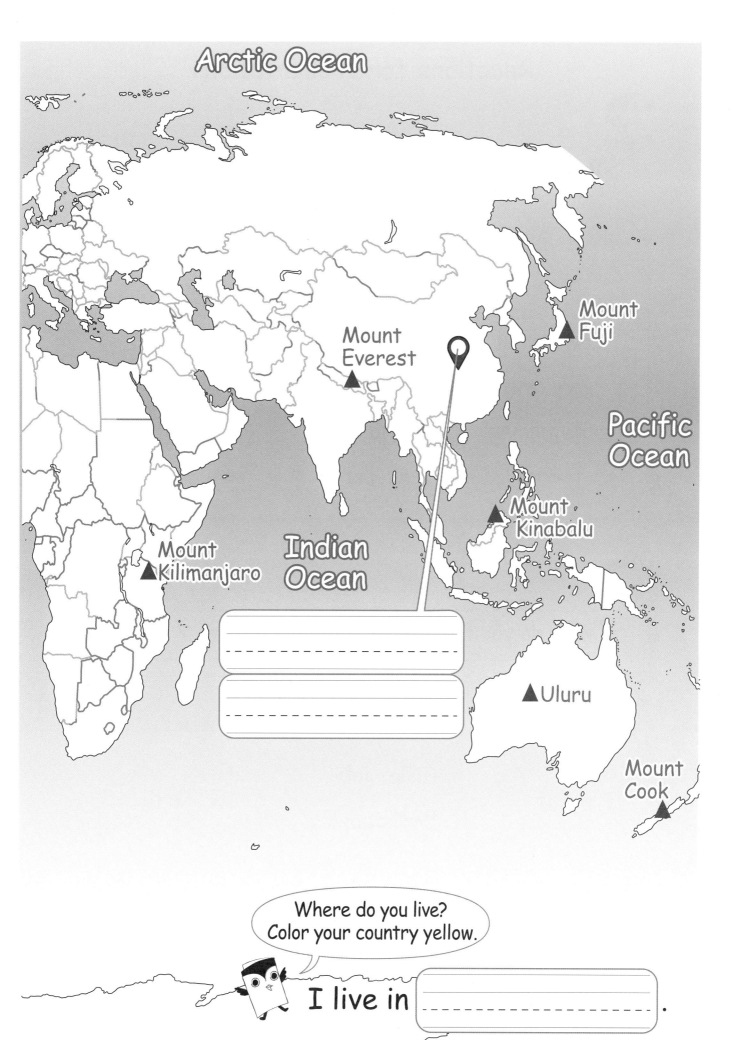

Arctic Ocean

Mount
Everest

Mount
Fuji

Pacific
Ocean

Mount
Kinabalu

Mount
Kilimanjaro

Indian
Ocean

▲Uluru

Mount
Cook

Where do you live?
Color your country yellow.

I live in

69

Reactions for Presentations

What do you think about the presentations?

I think your presentations is...

★★★★★

...awesome!   ...wonderful!

...brilliant!   ...marvelous!

...outstanding!   ...fantastic!

...terrific!   ...excellent!

★★★★☆

...very good!

...really nice!

...great!

...enjoyable!

How do you feel about the presentations?

★★★★★

I love it!

★★★★☆

Great job!

Well done!

★★★☆☆

I like it!

Interesting!   Super!   Neat!   Unique!

Cool!   Fun!   Nice!

Reactions for Interviews

Show your friends how you feel with reactions!

Thanks

Thank you.

You're welcome.

It's nothing.

No problem!

Agreement

I think so, too.

You're right.

Good point.

Me too.

I agree.

So do I.

That's true.

You are right!

Quite right!

Interest

Really?

Wow!

No way!

Cool!

Lucky you!

Disagreement

I'm not sure about that.

Yes, but...

Maybe...

You really think so?

Confirmation

That's sounds fun (interesting, etc.).

You could be right.

I'm happy to hear that.

How so?

I see.

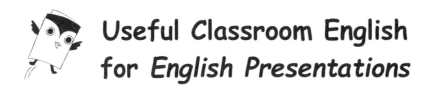

Useful Classroom English for *English Presentations*

☆ When you don't know the meaning...

What does "apple" mean?

It means "りんご."

☆ When you don't know the English word...

How do you say "りんご" in English?

We say "apple."

☆ When you don't know the spelling...

How do you spell "cat?"

C-A-T.

☆ When you need help...

Could you help me?

Sure!

☆ When you don't understand...

Could you say that again?

OK!

☆ When you have a question...

I have a question.

OK! Ask me.